caves, graves and catacombs

Natalie Jane Prior is fascinated by things buried and hidden – her other books in the True Stories series include *Bog Bodies* and *Mysterious Ruins*. Apart from archaeology, her interests include gardening, theater, science fiction and chocolate. She lives in Brisbane, Australia above ground, with her husband and bull terrier Ragnar.

Other great books in the **True Stories** series:
Bog Bodies
Mummies and Curious Corpses
by Natalie Jane Prior
The Cruellest Place on Earth
Stories from the Antarctic
by John Nicholson
Dance Crazy
Star Turns from Ballet to Belly Dancing
by Natalie Jane Prior
Monsters
And Creatures of the Night
by Sue Bursztynski
Mysterious Ruins
Lost Cities and Buried Treasure
by Natalie Jane Prior
Potions to Pulsars
Women doing Science
by Sue Bursztynski

caves, graves and catacombs

secrets from beneath the earth

Natalie Jane Prior

A LITTLE ARK BOOK

ALLEN & UNWIN

First published in 1996
A Little Ark Book. Allen & Unwin Pty Ltd
Distributed in the U.S.A. by Independent Publishers Group,
814 North Franklin Street, Chicago, IL. 60610, Phone 312 337 0747,
Fax 312 337 5985, Internet: ipgbook@mcs.com
Distributed in Canada by McClelland & Stewart,
481 University Avenue, Suite 900, Toronto, O.N. M5G 2E9,
Phone 416 598 1114, Fax 416 598 4002

10 9 8 7 6 5 4 3 2 1

National Library of Australia
cataloguing-in-publication entry:

Prior, Natalie Jane, 1963- .
    Caves, graves and catacombs.

    Bibliography.
    Includes index.
    ISBN 1 86448 096 3.

    1. Caves - Juvenile literature. 2. Underground areas - Juvenile
    literature. 3. Burial - Juvenile literature. I. Title. (Series: True
    stories (St Leonards, NSW).

620.4144

Photo credits
Royal Cave, Buchan: Coo-ee Picture Library
Gippsland worms: Wildlife Wonderland
Centennial Park Reservoir: NSW Water Board
lava stream: International Photographic Library
Roman catacombs: Coo-ee Picture Library (photo by G. Sommer)
Coober Pedy house: Peter Caust, Underground Books,
Coober Pedy
Cappadocian village: Paul Connor
Sleeping in Aldwych Tube station: Imperial War Museum, London
(photo by Associated Press)

Photo research by Catherine O'Rourke

Designed and typeset by Mark Carter
Printed by McPherson's Printing Group

Contents

Acknowledgments

Thanks to Sonja van den Ende for information about sewer safety, and to the Volcano World people for kindly answering my questions. Thank you to Rhodes Hart of Queensland University for information about underground nuclear tests — also to Margaret Connolly and Sarah Brenan, and to John Nicholson for finding the time to do yet another set of great illustrations.

The quotation on page 8 is from an Internet site for caving enthusiasts.

This book is for my father.

Introduction

This is a book about a world most people never stop to think about: the world beneath our feet.

The underground world is completely different to the one we are used to — strange, beautiful, dangerous and full of adventure. It is inhabited by creatures as alien-looking as any being from another planet. Humans, too, live and work there, building homes, shelters and hideaways in places where the daylight never reaches. The underground world is the world of buried treasure, of measureless, unexplored caves, of graveyards and catacombs filled with bones. Above all it is a world of darkness: cold, frightening, yet at the same time enticing.

Enter it — if you dare...

1 The Natural World of the Underground

The magical lure of caves

This is how one caver describes the excitement of going underground:

> A cave is a completely different and alien environment. It smells different, musty and earthy. Sounds are strangely muffled and close, yet bounce around and reverberate in the enclosed spaces. You're even dressed differently — usually tough, loose coveralls, knee pads, sometimes gloves, sturdy climbing shoes and a hardhat with lamp. You're carrying supplies, emergency equipment, ropes, climbing gear. The plant and animal life are almost surreal — bats, weird translucent slime molds, hairy tree roots, albino amphibians with huge eyes and visible internal organs, furry patches of fungus...

Cavers are brave and adventurous people. They must be very fit, strong, quick-witted and level-headed, with the ability to keep going even when they are exhausted. Inside a cave they may encounter sheer falls of rock, passages blocked by mud or water and tiny cracks in the rock through which they must squeeze to reach the next cavern, or even the surface. In a single expedition, a caver may be called upon to be a rappeller, scuba diver, rock climber, geographer and scientist: all in total darkness. The reward? Excitement, danger and, most of all, the thrill of experiencing a world few people ever get to see, an underground wilderness of strange and unimaginable beauty.

Caves are formed in different ways — some by the action of the sea beating against the coastline, others by glaciers scouring out rocky mountain slopes. Many caves form where the underlying rock is limestone. When rainwater seeps down it dissolves the limestone, and a cave gradually forms.

> **an underground wilderness of strange and unimaginable beauty**

Sometimes, when mineral-laden water drips from a cave roof, it crystalizes and forms either an icicle-like stalactite (which hangs from the cave roof) or a stalagmite on the cave floor. Other mysterious-looking mineral deposits found in caves include 'cave coral' made of calcium carbonate, which looks just like the coral found beneath the sea, and 'moonmilk'. Moonmilk looks rather like cheese and is a combination of mineral deposits and invisible, living **bacteria**.

Another type of cave or tunnel is the lava tube. Occasionally when a volcano erupts the lava flows down an old, dry river bed. Some of the lava sticks to the sides and floor of the river bed and hardens against it. The top also goes hard, because it is exposed to the cool outside air, but the lava in the middle keeps flowing, and eventually drains away, leaving a hollow tube. A famous system of lava tubes can be found at the extinct Undara volcano in north Queensland. In fact, the Undara lava tubes have helped astronomers from NASA understand similar geological features on the Moon.

Entrance to a lava tube

The only way to find out about caves is to explore them. Because caving is such a dangerous sport, it is important to plan an expedition carefully. Before they leave, cavers must make sure they have told somebody on the surface where the cave is, how many people are going, when the expedition is going to start, and the time they expect to return. Experienced cavers should always be present to help people who have never caved before, and make sure that the cave which is chosen for exploration is not too difficult for the party to manage. It is also important to have good-quality clothing and equipment, including climbing tackle, helmets and lamps. Finally, in case of an emergency, a caving party should be completely familiar with rescue procedures for any number of possible accidents. Each member of the party should have his or her own job, and be prepared to carry it out quickly and without panicking if the worst happens.

Usually the worst does not happen — most missing cavers have simply lost track of time underground and frightened people on the surface by not arriving back when they said they would. However, more serious accidents can and do occur. Like rock climbers and mountaineers, cavers can slip and be injured, or be hit by rock falls; like divers they can drown. Underground rivers can suddenly flood caverns and cut cavers off from the surface. Or someone can get stuck in a narrow passage or 'squeeze' — perhaps the passage was narrower than its entrance, or a large person got stuck after a smaller caver had passed safely through. In this situation, some cavers suggest using washing-up liquid as a lubricant to try and get the person out. Otherwise, hammers and chisels may have to be used to widen the passage.

> **Underground rivers can suddenly flood...**

Most cavers enjoy their expeditions to the underground world because they offer an exciting combination of sport and scientific exploration. However, caves are very fragile environments. A single careless caver can destroy beautiful mineral formations which have taken thousands of years to form, or disturb the habitats of cave-dwelling animals such as bats. Some caves have even been used as garbage dumps by thoughtless humans unaware of the delicate balance of nature inside.

Luckily, cavers are becoming increasingly aware of their responsibilities towards the underground environment, and most are now painstakingly careful. Many caves around the world have been declared National Parks, and some have been closed off to all visitors except scientists. Other caves, like the Waitomo Caves in New Zealand, have been popular tourist attractions for generations; they are monitored by ecologists to make sure that any human impact is kept to a minimum. If all cave visitors are careful, the world's great underground wildernesses will be preserved for cavers of the future to enjoy.

SOME CAVE FACTS AND FIGURES

- *Longest cave system*

	Mammoth Cave System, USA	348 miles long

- *Longest underwater cave*

	Nohoch Nah Chich, Mexico	24.5 miles

- *Biggest cave chamber*

	Sarawak Chamber, Malaysia	2297 feet long

- *Deepest cave* Reseau Jean Bernard, France   5256+ feet deep
- *Longest lava tube*

	Kazamura, Hawaii	16+ miles long

- *Longest stalactite*

	Cueva de Nerja, Spain	194 feet long

- *Tallest stalagmite*

	Krásnohorská, Slovakia	105 feet tall

The Witch of Wookey Hole

Stalagmites and stalactites are often the most spectacular features of limestone caves — and Wookey Hole, a famous cave in the English county of Somerset, has a stalagmite with an eerie legend attached to it. The gnarled, misshapen stalagmite looks a little like a hunched-over figure, and is known locally as 'The Witch of Wookey Hole'.

According to the legend, Wookey Hole was once inhabited by an evil witch. She cast spells on the local inhabitants, particularly young people in love. In her own youth, the witch had been spurned by her lover, and now she hated to see other people happy.

Eventually, news of the witch's spells reached nearby Glastonbury Abbey, where a brave young monk decided it was time to do something to stop her. Armed only with his faith in God and a small bottle of holy water, he set off for the cave, praying loudly as he went. As soon as the witch heard him coming, she knew she was done for. She gathered up her nanny goat and its kid, and tried to run away. But the monk was too quick for her. He snatched the bottle of holy water from his belt pouch, sprinkled it over the witch — and watched her turn to stone before his eyes.

Even though the witch was turned to stone, the local people never quite lost their fear of her. Dark tales about her evil deeds have lasted to this very day. When the makers of the TV show 'Doctor Who' visited the cave to film 'outer space' sequences in the 1970s, the actors were warned by

> watched her turn to stone before his eyes

guides to be respectful to the Witch. Some of them ignored the warning and poked fun at her. Within moments, the boat they were traveling in capsized, throwing them into the icy waters of the underground River Axe and nearly drowning them.

But was there any truth at all in the legend of the witch? Perhaps. In 1912, archaeologists excavating in the cavern discovered the ancient skeleton of a woman. Buried with her were a goat and a kid — and what might have been the remains of a crystal ball...

Cave discoveries

Human beings have always loved to explore, by boat, on foot and on horseback. The great explorers of the past spent centuries mapping out our world bit by bit, but today most of this work is done. People in search of adventure must look harder for uncharted wildernesses to explore. Like deep-sea divers and travelers to outer space, cavers are some of the last true adventurers and explorers in the world.

The greatest ambition of every caver is to discover a completely new cave: one in which no other person has ever stood before. Luckily for them, the world is full of unexplored caves, some of them full of wonderful geological formations or the bones of long-extinct animals. One of the most famous cave discoveries of recent times is the Sarawak Chamber on the island of Borneo. It was discovered in 1981 beneath an almost unexplored tract of mountainous jungle.

cavers are some of the last true adventurers and explorers

English cavers Andy Eavis, Dave Checkley and Tony White had no idea when they went underground that they would shortly make caving history. In fact they were almost at the end of their expedition, and planning to return to the surface with their newly completed cave maps, when the river passage they were following unexpectedly opened out into a huge underground chamber.

The three men found themselves in the midst of an enormous field of darkness. It was a frightening experience. The chamber was so huge that the light from their headlamps faded out into utter blackness. Unable to see the walls on any side, they could only find their way out by using their compasses.

Today, the three Englishmen's spectacular discovery has been properly mapped, and is famous as the world's biggest underground cavern. We now know that the Sarawak Chamber is 2297 feet long, ranges from 656 to 1410 feet wide, and is around 328 feet high. When the river passage on either side is taken into account, the entire cave is almost two miles in length!

The Sarawak Chamber is famous for its size. Other caves are exciting because of what they contain. One of the most famous collections of cave art in the world, at Altamira in northern Spain, was discovered by a small girl and her father in 1875. In fact it was the little girl who first saw and pointed out the animals which prehistoric people had painted on the walls as part of their magic hunting ritual. 'Look, Daddy — bulls!' she said. Later, experts were able to date the bulls to the Ice Age, 13,000 years ago.

> **frozen waterfalls, ice stalactites, and glittering curtains of green ice**

Like the paintings at Altamira, many of the greatest cave discoveries of all time have been made by accident. In 1994, a party of cavers exploring in Honduras in Central America slipped through a crack in the rock and discovered a cave full of human bones: an ancient cemetery containing as many as 200 people! The fragile bones were mostly stacked in groups around tiny natural pools of water, and were furry with mineral deposits. The magical Dachstein Ice Cave — now one of Austria's most popular tourist attractions — was discovered in 1910 by a local man when he was caught out in a thunderstorm. Taking refuge in a cave entrance, he quickly realized that it penetrated far deeper into the mountain than anyone could tell from outside. Soon a party of experienced cavers was exploring breathtakingly beautiful galleries made of glacial ice: frozen waterfalls, ice stalactites, and glittering curtains of green ice which reflected their lantern-light like huge natural crystals.

DID YOU KNOW?
• In the days before refrigerators, keeping food cool was often a problem. The people of the Swiss Alps often solved the problem by storing their cheeses and other perishables in nature's own refrigerators — ice caves!

Howling caves

The mediaeval chronicler Henry of Huntingdon made a list of the 'Wonders of England' in 1135. Among them was a 'howling cave' which wailed and moaned when visitors entered it.

Modern speleologists (people who study caves) think this may have been the Peak Cavern. When strong winds blow through the cave they echo off its walls and make an eerie sound which does sound rather like a howl.

The miraculous cave of Lourdes

One of the most famous caves in the world is at Lourdes, France. The cave itself is nothing special — but in 1858, a series of remarkable events turned it into one of the most visited places in France.

Bernadette Soubirous was a quiet, gentle fourteen-year-old girl most people never looked twice at. But when she visited the cave or grotto on the bank of the River Gave, a beautiful young woman mysteriously appeared to her, eventually revealing herself as Jesus' mother, the Virgin Mary. Bernadette's visions quickly turned her into a celebrity, but she was a humble, devout person and hated the publicity. She joined a nearby convent, where she lived the rest of her short life in peace. In 1933, she was officially made a saint of the Roman Catholic Church.

The cave where Bernadette had her visions is still there, but today it is a very different place. Every year, four million sick people come from all over the world to visit the spring of water in the grotto, hoping their faith and prayers will make them well again. Many of the cures reported at Lourdes have been checked by doctors, and do seem to be miraculous. Bernadette's grotto is one of the most famous places of healing in the world.

Plants and animals in the dark

From the world's hottest deserts to the icy polar wastes, animals have made homes in the most unlikely places — and some of the strangest creatures on the planet can be found underground.

Enter a cave, and you enter a whole new world. Inside the entrance, close to the surface, are animals which look much like the ones you are familiar with. Owls, bats, snakes, spiders and insects live on the twilight verges, sometimes leaving the cave at night to hunt abroad. But venture deeper into the cave, and you will encounter a world of total darkness, almost without sound; a cold world inhabited by giant beetles, weird fish without eyes, and bats which rely on **sonar** to find their way about in the darkness.

There are 950 species of bats, which scientists divide into two main groups, megabats and microbats. Megabats usually feed on fruit and roost out in the open. The cave-dwelling bats are microbats, and they are much smaller, with bodies about the size of a mouse's.

giant beetles, weird fish without eyes, bats...

Most bats eat insects, but there is a variety which catches fish and the Australian ghost bat or false-vampire bat, the largest of the microbats, hunts mice, frogs, birds, lizards and even other bats. The true

Australian ghost bat or false-vampire bat

vampire bats live in South America. They make a small bite in the skin of animals like pigs or cows and lap the blood with their tongues. They don't take enough blood to damage the animal, but some of them carry a disease called rabies and this can be a problem.

Animals like bats spend part of their lives in caves, and part of it in the outside world. Other animals like to live in caves if they can, but can also manage in suitable places outside. Animals that live permanently in caves dwell in complete darkness, finding ways to eat and move about which do not involve seeing. They also have to cope with constant dampness and a low temperature (caves are usually very cold places).

Cave animals are often very peculiar-looking. Many of them have no eyes (or small and useless ones), and rely on other senses such as touch and hearing to find their way about. They also tend to be skinny and stretched-out-looking, with colorless skin or fur. In fact, some fish living in underground rivers are so colorless they are almost see-through! But they are not the only nightmarish-looking creatures to be found in the permanent darkness. Horror stories of giant underground beetles are not entirely made up: many underground insects are much bigger than their cousins on the surface.

Not all underground animals are horrible-looking. One of the most beautiful and unusual of all cave animals is the glowworm. This is not really a worm, but the larva of a fly-like insect called the fungus gnat which lives in Australia and New Zealand. (Insects called glowworms in Europe are really beetles.) In New Zealand, the Waitomo Caves are famous for their glowworms, and tourists from all over the world make special trips by boat along an underground river to see them. The walls and ceiling of the Glowworm Cave shimmer with a mystical blue-green light that is made by thousands upon thousands of tiny animals.

Glowworms like to live in dark, damp, rocky places, so they can also be seen outside caves. But while they look eerie, the reason for their light is both natural and very practical. The glow (called bio-luminescence) is produced by a chemical reaction inside the glowworm's body, and is used to attract the tiny insects it feeds on. The brightest glowworm is always the hungriest. Like a spider spinning a web, it finds a suitable spot on the cave ceiling, and exudes sticky threads or filaments from its body. When the victim flies towards the light, it is trapped and paralyzed by them. The greedy glowworm then pulls up the thread and bites its victim's head off.

> **The brightest glowworm is always the hungriest**

Wonder worms

Not all underground animals live in caves. One of the commonest — and friendliest — of all underground animals is the humble earthworm.

Clever gardeners know that an army of worms in the vegetable patch is worth hours with a fork and shovel. As a worm pushes through the earth, soil enters its 'mouth' and passes through its tube-like body; the worm takes nutrients from the soil, and pushes what is left out the other end. This means that a worm 'poos' its own body weight once a day! In the process, it breaks up the soil, making it easier for water to penetrate deeply, and for growing plants to send down roots.

Another curious fact about earthworms is that they are hermaphrodites, which means that they are both male and female. However, an earthworm cannot produce offspring by itself. Instead, it mates with another worm and produces an egg capsule which later hatches out baby worms.

> **DID YOU KNOW?**
> • The biggest living thing in the world is a huge underground fungus in the United States. The honey fungus (*Armillaria bubosa*) covers 1500 acres of Washington State and is between 500 and 1000 years old.

Wildflowers underground

Western Australia is famous for its wild flowers. Every spring thousands of tourists travel there to see them. But there is one native flower few visitors will ever get to see: a type of orchid called Rhizanthella.

Finding a Rhizanthella is extremely difficult, as it grows and flowers completely underground. Its flowers are tiny — some are only a centimetre across — but very beautiful, and sweetly scented. Although it is an orchid, and not a fungus, the Rhizanthella feeds off other plants to live. A fungus called Rhizoctamia links it to its favorite food, a native shrub called the broom honey myrtle.

Underground orchids are very rare: so rare, in fact, that for years they were thought to be extinct. Today botanists from the University of Western Australia keep careful track of only 250 plants, found with the help of the Landsat satellite, which pinpointed the most likely areas for them to search.

> **250 plants, found with the help of the Landsat satellite**

Volcanoes: fire from under the earth

One day in 1943, a Mexican farmer called Dionisio Pulido noticed a strange crack in his cornfield. The crack was about 20 inches deep, and ran through the middle of a deep hole which he had been using as his personal garbage dump. The earth shook and started lifting along the crack, and then suddenly the air was filled with a foul stink like rotten eggs. Dionisio gathered up his family and fled in terror. The next day, when he ventured back to investigate, he found a baby volcano, 33 feet tall, smoking and popping and spewing out ash in the middle of the cornfield. It eventually grew to 1102 feet tall and swallowed a nearby village.

a baby volcano, 33 feet tall, smoking and popping and spewing out ash

Of all the world's underground dangers, volcanoes are the most spectacular and deadly. For years a volcano will slumber peacefully, fooling local inhabitants into thinking it is just like any other mountain. Then semi-molten rock called magma will start moving deep in the earth. Gas builds up inside it, forcing it to expand, and start creeping to the surface. The earth may start to tremble, and poisonous gas might be released. Eventually — perhaps with a violent explosion — the magma bursts through the earth's surface. Volcanoes tend to change dramatically from one eruption to the next. They can have their entire tops blown off, or they can grow spectacularly when ash or lava (magma which has reached the surface) accumulates and solidifies on the slopes. This happened with Parícutin, Dionisio Pulido's baby volcano.

Diagram showing how lava forces its way up from the depths of the earth

Today the earth has about 1,500 active volcanoes, though some of these have not erupted for hundreds or even thousands of years. Most of them are found along the 'Ring of Fire', which encircles the Pacific Ocean, passing through places like Japan, Indonesia, New Zealand, and the western coasts of North and South America.

Many volcanoes erupt underneath the ocean. In 1963, the people of Iceland were startled when a new island, Surtsey, mysteriously appeared off their coast. It was a volcano which had been erupting under the sea, and had gradually grown tall enough to be seen. Easter Island, in the Pacific Ocean, is a famous volcanic island formed long ago.

People have always been in awe of volcanoes. The people of Hawaii, for example, believed for centuries that the **crater** of Kilauea was inhabited by the goddess Pélé, who caused the volcano to erupt when she lost her temper. The Hawaiian queen, Kapiolani, became a Christian in the 1820s. Despite the terrified pleadings of her subjects, she marched over 100 miles to the volcano and climbed down into its crater. Watched by about 80 companions, she challenged the goddess to kill her, and contemptuously hurled lumps of lava into the sacred fires. When Pélé was silent, many Hawaiians lost their faith in her, and became Christians like their queen.

Odd as it may seem, people have often deliberately chosen to live close to volcanoes. Volcanic soil is rich, fertile and easy to farm, and when the volcano doesn't erupt for years, it is easy to forget about the risk. This is exactly what happened in the famous eruption of Mt. Vesuvius in Italy: convinced the volcano was extinct, many wealthy Romans actually built their villas on its slopes! An eruption in 79 A.D. killed about 2000 people and buried the nearby towns of Herculaneum and Pompeii, turning them into time capsules for archaeologists to dig up centuries later.

Over the centuries, many people have died in volcanic eruptions. When the volcanic island of Krakatoa in Indonesia blew up in 1883, 36,000 people perished in a tidal wave; more recently, in 1985, 22,000 people were buried by volcanic mud flows in Colombia. Ash falls and poison gas are the other main causes of death in an eruption. (Although it is as hot as 1832-2147°F, few people are actually killed by lava, as it moves comparatively slowly.) Even experienced vulcanologists (scientists who specialize in studying volcanoes) can misjudge the risks. In 1991, the French husband-and-wife team Maurice and Katia Krafft died tragically while studying an eruption of the Japanese volcano, Unzen.

> **time capsules for archaeologists to dig up centuries later**

Today many volcanoes are monitored by vulcanologists, who try to predict when an eruption is on its way. One such prediction was made at Rabaul, in Papua New Guinea in September 1994. Rabaul is one of the most dangerously situated towns in the whole world: it is actually *inside* a caldera (collapsed volcano). But when two nearby cones started erupting, the vulcanologists were prepared. Fifty thousand people were evacuated — and although much of Rabaul was destroyed, only five inhabitants died.

Volcano suicides

Empedocles was a famous philosopher who lived nearly 2,500 years ago. Fascinated by the way the earth was made up, he spent long hours on the slopes of Mt. Etna in southern Italy. Eventually, in a state of despair, he threw himself into its crater.

A rash of volcano suicides occurred in Japan earlier in this century. Spurred on by the death of a schoolgirl who jumped into the crater of the volcano Mihara-yama in 1933, an incredible 1208 people tried to hurl themselves to their deaths. So many of these suicide attempts were successful that the authorities eventually decided it would be a good idea to build a fence.

The mystery of the earth's center

One of the earliest science fiction writers was Jules Verne, a nineteenth-century Frenchman with an insatiable curiosity about the world and its wonders. In his book *Journey to the Center of the Earth,* Verne

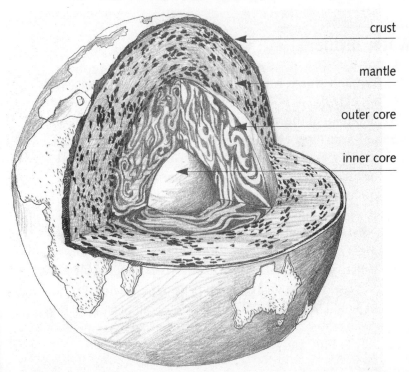

crust

mantle

outer core

inner core

describes how a party of travelers enters a volcano in Iceland and makes its way to the very center of the Earth. Here they are caught up in a volcanic eruption, and spewed safely back up to the surface. *Journey to the Center of the Earth* was an instant bestseller, and many years later it was turned into a successful movie.

In real life Jules Verne's underground travelers would not have had nearly so much luck. Modern geologists tell us that the Earth is made up of four main layers: the crust or outermost layer, the mantle, the outer core (made of molten rock) and the inner core. The core, which is solid, is about 3720 miles deep and has a temperature of about 8312°F.

Water diviners

Without water, human beings, animals and plants will quickly die; it is vital for our survival. Yet when we look at a map of the world, we see salt oceans covering most of its surface. Usable fresh water, in rivers and lakes, is much less plentiful. But there is another source that ordinary maps don't show — water locked away underground.

For thousands of years, humans have dug wells to get underground water. But how do they know where to dig? Geologists who specialize in the study of underground water can give some clues about where to look: but their services are expensive and not always available, especially in poor Third World countries where the need for fresh clean water is often desperate. Luckily, there is another way to find water when it is hidden underground.

Water diviners, or 'dowsers', practice an art which is thousands of years old. Holding simple tools — a forked stick, a weight on a string or two metal rods — lightly in their hands, they pace out a piece of land. If they pass over a hidden underground spring, or a stream of groundwater running through a fault in the rock, mysterious things start to happen. The forked stick suddenly jerks downwards, pointing to the place where the water is. The weight spins on its string. Or the metal rods start swaying in the dowser's hands, crossing over each other to form an 'X'. When this happens, water has been found — the dowser's work is done and the well-diggers can take over. Some dowsers are so skilled that they can even tell their customers how deep they will have to dig before they reach the water!

Because dowsing seems very mysterious, dowsers have sometimes been feared, and accused of being witches or magicians. In the United States dowsing is traditionally known as 'water witching'. But dowsing is not 'magic'. It is simply something which works, but which nobody really understands properly. In the past when most dowsers used light and springy forked sticks (usually from rowan or hazel bushes), one popular theory was that the wood was 'thirsty' for the water. When the dowser walked over an underground spring or stream, the rod jerked downwards because it wanted to get at the water. Most modern dowsers reject this theory, and prefer to use pendulums or metal rods instead of the forked stick. They suggest that our bodies are much more sensitive than we think. While we may not see an underground water source, our bodies sense its presence and react to it. Holding a rod or pendulum simply makes the dowser's body reaction easy to see.

Some dowsers work full-time at their craft, and are so confident in their abilities that they promise to refund the customer's drilling costs if water is not found. (The average dowser finds water four out of five times, but one British dowser was so talented he had a success rate of 97 per cent, finding water almost every time he looked for it.) Dowsers are employed by farmers' support groups, and by water and sewerage authorities around the world. In America, dowsers are even known to specialize in locating old sewerage pipes which are not marked on street plans. Dowsing has also been important in times of war. During World War I, an Australian soldier called Sapper Kelly became famous when he found 32 new wells in a single week. By finding clean, fresh water for troops serving in Turkey, he helped them avoid terrible water-borne diseases such as cholera.

How does somebody become a dowser? Dowsers say that almost everybody can dowse successfully to some extent, but that some people are better at it than others. Some dowsers even search for gold and other precious metals rather than water. And some of the most talented dowsers claim they do not even have to leave their homes to find underground water. They sit in front of a map spread out on a table and dangle a pendulum over it. When the pendulum moves, the dowser marks a cross on the map to show where the well should be dug.

2 Graves, Crypts and Catacombs

Buried alive!

Imagine waking up from a deep sleep and finding yourself unable to move. You're lying on your back, your legs are stretched out straight, your hands are folded across your breast. Sheets are wrapped tightly around your body and your face. You try to pull them off and sit up, and find you can't — you're boxed in, in suffocating blackness. You open your mouth to scream, and then realize that no one will hear you. You have been buried alive...

For centuries, people reading horror novels have been terrified by stories like this. Today, sophisticated medical equipment means that when doctors say somebody is dead, they really are dead. But diagnosing death has not always been so easy. As recently as 100 years ago, attendants at a death bed would hold mirrors up to a dying person's mouth to see if any breath would mist the glass. There were other ways of telling whether somebody was dead. You could lay a feather across the lips to see if it would stir, or prick the skin with a sharp pin or scalpel to try and provoke a scream. Tricks like these seem strange, but were very important. Without modern stethoscopes or monitors to scan brain activity, there was always the chance that a very sick person with a faint heartbeat might be mistaken for a corpse, and sent off to the local cemetery.

What were the chances of being buried alive? Very occasionally, some people may have been, particularly during disease epidemics when there were a lot of deaths. With diseases like cholera or bubonic plague on the rampage, it was important to bury bodies quickly so that they would not infect living people. Deep faints or comas could also be mistaken for death, even by doctors. In one account of a funeral which happened on Australia's Darling Downs at the turn of this century, the dead man's friends and family were holding a wake, or party, around his **coffin**, when the 'corpse' sat up and frightened them half to death!

> the 'corpse' sat up and frightened them half to death!

Another very famous story concerns an eighteenth-century noblewoman who came back to life when a thief entered the family crypt and broke open her coffin. She woke up to find him stealing a gold ring from her finger — it is hard to imagine who had the greater fright, the lady or the burglar! So many versions of this legend are told that it is difficult to know whether it was ever true or not. Later on, during the nineteenth century, people became so scared of being buried alive that they invented all sorts of peculiar gadgets to give themselves a chance of surviving. One device was a bell hung from a tripod, which sat on top of the coffin while it lay awaiting burial. A piece of string was attached to the bell, threaded through a hole in the top of the coffin, and tied to the corpse's finger. If the dead person came back to life, all he or she had to do was ring the bell, and somebody would let them out.

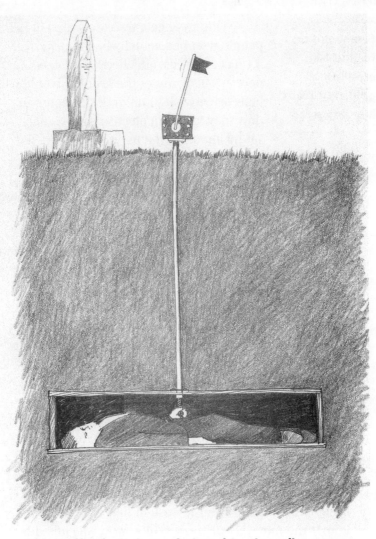

This 'coffin device' was designed to give a live person who had been accidentally buried a way of contacting friends above ground. A switch near the person's hand waves a flag on the surface

> **She woke up to find him stealing a gold ring from her finger...**

Other gadgets were designed to help people who had actually been buried. Strings and rods, attached to the dead person's body under the ground, would ring bells or wave flags up in the cemetery if they moved. Or an electric wire would sound an alarm if a button were pressed. (A modern, electronic version of this type of alarm has recently been put on the market in Italy.) The grave-digger would then hastily dig up the coffin. Unfortunately, most of these coffin alarms did not work the way they were supposed to, because it is normal for dead bodies to move when they are decomposing. Gases build up inside and sometimes burst the skin, something which would be more than enough to set off a sensitive alarm.

The safest way of making sure that someone was really dead before their burial was to wait until the body started to decompose. For this reason, it was common to wait several days before holding a funeral. Needless to say, in practically every case, the corpse failed to wake up.

Meanwhile, 'live burials' found their way into dozens of books and horror stories. A favorite character in early horror novels was the 'walled-up nun'. In the novels (and very occasionally, in real life) a nun who had been unfaithful to her vows would be bricked up alive in a corner of the convent cellar, with only a tiny loaf of bread and a jug of water to sustain her. Everybody knows the fairy tale of Snow White, who was jolted back into life when the seven dwarves moved her glass coffin and dislodged the piece of poisoned apple caught in her throat. And one of the most famous of all live burials can be found in Shakespeare's play *Romeo and Juliet*.

In the play, when Juliet's parents threaten to marry her off to a man she doesn't love, she doses herself with a drug which leaves her unconscious. Her parents think she is dead, and place her 'body' in the family **crypt.** Juliet's plan is for Romeo to rescue her, but her message reaches him too late. Romeo visits her grave, sees her lying dead, and kills himself by drinking poison — minutes before the 'corpse' wakes up out of her trance. Overcome by grief at the sight of Romeo's body, Juliet then stabs herself and the play ends, tragically with two real funerals.

Homes for bones: catacombs and charnel-houses

Think of all the people who have ever lived. Every single one of them has had to die, and every single body has

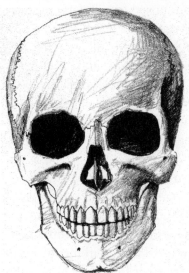

had to be disposed of. Our earth is crowded with the bones of dead human beings: like one enormous graveyard.

Nowadays, cremating or burning bodies is a common practice, and overcrowded graveyards are rarely seen. In Australia, where there is lots of space, a full cemetery is simply closed, and a new one opened elsewhere. But what of towns in Europe, that have many more people and less empty land? Their custom is for graves to be re-used, over and over again. Dead people are buried, and their families put up gravestones to remember them by. After a period of time, perhaps 50 or 100 years later when friends and family are dead too, the headstone is knocked down, the bones of the dead person are dug up, and a new corpse is buried in the same place.

This may seem disrespectful, but it is

> **thousands of dead bodies were buried in niches in the walls of maze-like tunnels under the city**

really the only sensible choice. In past centuries, overcrowded graveyards were filthy and dangerous places, where visitors were likely to catch fatal diseases from dead bodies which were literally bursting out of the ground. (The terrible bubonic plague or 'Black Death' which hit England in 1665 is supposed to have started in a London graveyard, St. Giles.) Besides, when a grave is cleared out the skeleton is not just thrown out as if it were rubbish. It is taken away, and carefully placed with other bones in a special crypt or room known as an ossuary, bone-house or charnel-house (the word ossuary comes from the Latin for 'bone'). Ossuaries exist all over Europe, and some can still be seen by visitors today.

A famous example of an ossuary on a grand scale is the Paris Catacombs. A catacomb is an underground burial place or cemetery, and the most famous ones were built in Rome from about 200 A.D. to 400 A.D. Here, thousands of dead bodies were buried in niches in the walls of maze-like tunnels under the city. The Paris

Catacombs were built nearly 1600 years after the ones in Rome, but the basic idea behind them was the same. Like the ancient Romans, eighteenth-century Parisians wanted to put their cemetery under the ground and out of the way. The only difference was that the people of Paris actually dug up an existing cemetery, and moved all the bones into the catacombs.

Two hundred years ago, Paris had only one cemetery, known as Les Innocents. It was overcrowded, frightening and dangerous. One eighteenth-century visitor to Les Innocents was an English traveler called William Cole. He said it was 'one of the most filthy and nasty places I ever was in', and described how he peered into a pit, about 97 square feet, which was full of badly made coffins and rotten, stinking corpses. Cole claimed that the stench from the dead bodies was still hanging around him for days after his visit.

Needless to say, the French authorities were also concerned. Leaving dead bodies lying around was not only unpleasant: it was unhygienic, and bred all sorts of terrible diseases. In 1786, Les Innocents was closed for good, and plans were drawn up to replace the old graveyard with a marketplace. But what was to be done with all the millions of bones which had accumulated in Les Innocents over the centuries?

piles of legs, arms and skulls

The authorities quickly came up with a solution. Just outside old Paris were some ancient quarries, long since abandoned. The quarries went deep into the ground, and could be turned into a huge subterranean catacomb or charnel-house — in other words, a final resting place for the bones. In April 1787,

BURIED IN GOLD

Attila the Hun was a savage barbarian king who terrorized Europe in the fifth century A.D. After he died suddenly at his own wedding in 453 A.D., his followers prepared a strange burial for him. They sealed his body in three coffins, one inside the other — one of pure gold, one of silver and one of iron — which they placed at the bottom of a deep hole. The grave was then almost completely filled with gold: money, plate and jewelry, which Attila had plundered in the course of his many wars. Finally, the top part of the grave shaft was filled with earth and leveled so that nobody could see where it was.

After Attila's burial, all the men who had witnessed it were executed in case they went back to dig up the treasure. No one has seen it since. Attila's blood-soaked gold still lies waiting for the someone brave enough to disturb his rest.

workmen started digging up layer upon layer of graves in Les Innocents, and transferring the bones they found to their new home in the quarry. Of course, after so long it was impossible to tell which skeleton was which, so when the cartloads of bones arrived, more workers were employed to sort them out into piles of legs, arms and skulls. These were stacked neatly into piles to preserve space. This grisly work took over a year to complete.

Nobody knows exactly how many skeletons lie within the Paris catacombs, but it is somewhere between three and six million. Perhaps because the work of stacking the bones was so hard and unpleasant (and scary — imagine lugging sacks of skeletons through underground passages, with only a feeble lantern to light your way), the workers sometimes stacked them in

the catacombs became a tourist attraction!

weird patterns. They made pyramids of skulls, and left 'skull and crossbones' in odd places to scare the unwary visitors who were soon roaming the tunnels. In fact, news of the vast complex of bone-filled tunnels spread so quickly that the catacombs became a tourist attraction! On special days, visitors would go down 90 steps into the winding tunnels underneath the bustling city, and wonder about the identity of the people whose skeletons they saw there (visitors to Paris can still see them). Horror writers wrote terrifying stories about the place, and the catacombs passed into underground legend...

Grave-robbers

too many doctors and not enough villains

Trainee doctors and nurses need to learn about the way the human body is put together, and the best way of doing this is to dissect or cut open dead bodies. Nowadays, it is common for people to bequeath their bodies to medical schools in their wills, so that students can learn anatomy. But doctors in earlier days had to do their research in a much more grisly fashion.

According to the laws in England before 1832, dead criminals who had been executed would be handed over to surgeons and anatomy teachers to dissect. The only problem was, there were too many doctors and not enough villains. Ordinary people did not like the idea of their bodies being cut up, so the doctors were in a quandary. Their only solution to the problem of finding newly dead corpses was a grim one — they turned for help to local grave-robbers, also known as 'body-snatchers' or 'resurrectionists'.

Resurrectionists would keep an eye on the local cemeteries, and watch out for new burials. When a surgeon approached them for a corpse to dissect they would steal into the graveyard at midnight, leaving one person, perhaps a small boy, as lookout. Working silently in gangs, they would dig down swiftly into the newly turned earth, using wooden shovels which made as little noise as possible. When they reached the coffin they would break open the lid, unwrap the body from its **shroud** and bundle it into a wheelbarrow or handcart so that it could be taken away to where the customer was waiting. (Leaving the shroud behind was important, because if the grave-robbers took it, they could be accused of stealing as well as desecrating a grave.) Although robbing graves must have been frightening as well as disgusting work, it was worth it to poor and desperate men. An ordinary body in good condition would cost the doctor about eight golden guineas — in those days a lot of money.

Relatives of dead people took all sorts of precautions to make sure the newly buried bodies remained safe. For weeks after the person's death they would guard the grave at night; or they would fix alarms to warn the **sexton** of intruders. Rich people would bury their dead in huge stone vaults, while poor people, whose graves were most at risk, might fill them with quicklime, which made the bodies rot down quickly. One man even invented a patent iron coffin, designed to be unopenable by the most cunning resurrectionists in the business. But a determined grave-robber was usually unstoppable. One favorite trick was to pose as a grave-digger come to fill in the grave. The robber would quickly open the coffin, drop the dead body into a sack and fill the grave with earth — leaving behind an empty coffin. In many cases, the grieving relatives were not even aware that the body had been stolen.

Once the body was dug up, it had to be shipped off to the customer without delay. To be found with a 'resurrected' corpse was dangerous: caught out by furious members of the public, a grave-robber could expect little mercy, and would usually be beaten to within an inch of his life. The body was likely to rot if left out in the open for too long: for this reason, most body-snatching was done in cold weather, when corpses decayed more slowly. However, if the body were in good enough condition, the grave-robbers often waited long enough to pull out the teeth. These would be sold off separately to dentists to turn into dentures.

> **most body-snatching was done in cold weather**

For many years people in England were both repelled and fascinated by grave-robbing (the famous novelist Charles Dickens includes a gruesome account in his novel *A Tale of Two Cities*). Eventually however, a series of grisly murders in Edinburgh prompted the authorities to take action. In 1832, an Act of Parliament ordered that the bodies of poor people who died destitute in workhouses would be handed over to medical schools for dissection. While this was very unfair on poor people who did not want their bodies to be dissected, it did increase the supply of corpses, and stopped the gruesome trade of body-snatching for good.

The poems in the coffin

One of the most grisly stories in the history of literature concerns the English poet and painter, Dante Gabriel Rossetti. In 1860, after a long engagement, he married one of his models, a beautiful red-haired woman called Elizabeth (Lizzie) Siddal. Lizzie too was a talented artist and poet, but her husband neglected her, and the marriage was not a happy one.

Lizzie was sick and often in pain from what may have been tuberculosis, a deadly lung disease. She also suffered from depression. Her doctors prescribed laudanum, a powerful medicine which is made from opium poppies, like modern morphine (and heroin). Soon Lizzie became addicted to it. Every day she drank huge amounts which would have killed a normal person. Finally, in February 1862, Lizzie died very mysteriously. The official report said she had accidentally taken an overdose of laudanum, but rumors soon started to circulate that she had killed herself, and that a friend had destroyed her suicide note to prevent a scandal.

> **The notebook contained all his best and most beautiful poems**

Dante Gabriel Rossetti was beside himself with grief. Perhaps he knew Lizzie really had killed herself, and felt guilty because he had not been a better husband. At any rate, he now decided to prove how much he loved her. Just before Lizzie was nailed up in her coffin, Rossetti tucked a notebook inside with her. The notebook contained all his best and most beautiful poems — and it was the only copy he had.

Soon after this, Lizzie was buried in the Rossetti

family grave in London's Highgate Cemetery. Her unhappy life was over, but even in death she was not allowed to lie peacefully. After a while, Rossetti's thoughts turned to the notebook he had put inside her coffin. Now that life was starting to get back to normal, he couldn't help remembering how good the poems were. If he published them, they would make a fantastic collection. Perhaps he would even make some money from them. The problem was, how was he to get them back when they were buried underground in Lizzie's coffin?

For nearly seven years, Rossetti agonized over his beautiful poems. He knew that the only way to retrieve them was to dig up poor Lizzie's coffin, open it, and take out the notebook. The thought was horrible, but for Rossetti the prospect of losing his poems forever was worse. Lizzie had been a poet herself, Rossetti told himself sternly. She would have understood his dilemma. At last, in 1868, Rossetti came to a decision. He went to the Home Office, and applied for a government permit to exhume his wife's body from her grave.

At first, the people at the Home Office were difficult about giving Rossetti the permit. They said that the family grave belonged to his mother, not to him, and that he had to have her authority to dig it up. But eventually they gave permission for Lizzie's body to be exhumed. Rossetti couldn't bring himself to go to the cemetery, so he sent a friend instead. On a dark night in October 1869, the grave-diggers put up a huge tent over the Rossetti grave, and lit a fire to provide light for them to work by. Supervised by **undertakers,** and watched by a doctor, a lawyer and Rossetti's friend, the men dug down until they reached Lizzie's coffin. They broke open the lid, and brought the precious notebook of poems back to the surface.

Seven years in a cold, damp grave with a rotting corpse had left the notebook in rather bad condition. It smelled disgusting, and there was a huge worm-hole right through the middle of one of the poems, but luckily most of the pages were still quite readable. Rossetti's friend made sure the notebook was cleaned, disinfected and dried out before he gave it back. When the anxious widower enquired what his wife's body had been like, the friend kindly told him that she looked just as she had on the day she had been buried, and that her long red hair was as bright and lovely as ever.

After years in the ground, Lizzie's body was probably in worse shape than the notebook, but Rossetti preferred to believe what his friend told him. He settled down to work on editing the poems in the smelly notebook for publication, and somehow managed to finish the job. He had hoped to keep the grisly story of the poems' hiding place to himself, but it was impossible to stop the secret from spreading. Before long it was all over London. Some people were disgusted, some were pleased that the poems had been saved. One thing was for certain: everybody wanted to read them!

> **He had hoped to keep the grisly story of the poems' hiding place to himself**

The poems that had spent seven years hidden in a coffin made their author the magnificent sum of £800. But Dante Gabriel Rossetti never quite got over the experience. When he died, 20 years after Lizzie, he left very definite instructions that he was not to be buried at Highgate Cemetery.

Visiting a cemetery

Although some people think cemeteries (graveyards) are morbid or even scary, they are actually very interesting places to visit. Cemeteries are full of fascinating information about the past, and are often visited by historians searching for facts about a particular area or time.

Headstones in cemeteries can tell us about wars or disease epidemics which killed lots of people. Big expensive graves like ones seen in gold-rush towns tell us that a district was once very prosperous. And individual gravestones are interesting because they often contain the life stories of the people who are buried beneath them.

The best cemeteries to visit are old ones, as modern graveyards can have many very similar-looking headstones which don't contain much information. The big cemeteries in capital cities are full of fascinating (and sometimes peculiar)

DID YOU KNOW?

• Old graveyards are often arranged so that the graves run east to west. The dead person is buried with his/her head to the east (where the sun comes up) and feet to the west (where it 'dies' or sets). This tradition is very ancient, and dates back to the ancient Egyptians, who always made sure they buried their dead on the *west* bank of the Nile River, never on the east. You might like to take your compass with you when you next go to a graveyard, to check which direction the graves are laid out in.

monuments. (One grave in Brisbane, Australia, is shaped like a miniature boxing ring with a pair of stone boxing gloves on the headstone!) If you live in a small town, you will be sure to find many of the pioneers of your district buried in your local cemetery, or perhaps even a local celebrity or great-grandparent.

Here are a few things for cemetery explorers to look out for.

Angels and cherubs are some of the most popular monuments found in old graveyards. (Sadly, they are easily broken, and are often headless or wingless.) Cherubs, which look like chubby babies with wings, are often found on the graves of small children and babies.

Broken columns usually mean that the life of the person buried in the grave was cut short. They are often found on the graves of young people, or people who died suddenly or unexpectedly. (A broken column looks like a tall pillar cut off halfway.)

Chest tombs are shaped like huge above-ground stone boxes. However, this does not mean that the dead person is buried 'above ground'. In fact, they are buried underground in the usual way, and the stone 'tomb' is empty. (A famous exception to this can be found in the old New Orleans cemetery. Because the area was swampy and it was difficult to dig graves, early settlers learned to build them above ground. The cemetery is now a tourist attraction.)

Clasped hands can often be seen on old tombstones. They were popular on double husband-and-wife graves, and were meant to suggest that even though the couple were dead they were not parted. When only one person is buried in the grave the hands suggest that the dead person will meet his or her loved one again some day in the future.

Crosses mean that the person buried there was a Christian. Christians believe that Jesus was killed by being nailed to a cross, but that he later rose from the dead. The cross symbolizes that the dead person, too, will live again.

Doves are a Christian symbol for peace, and tell cemetery visitors that the dead person is now 'at peace'.

Family graves contain several members of one family. Old family graves, dating from the days when medicine was not as good and people did not live as long, are often filled with the remains of children who died young or as babies. They are quite large, and usually consist of two grave plots side by side.

Inscriptions on a gravestone usually tell us who is buried there, when they were born and when they died. They may also give information about where the person was born, what they died of, who their relations were (especially if they paid for the stone!) or what they did for a living. For this reason, local historians and genealogists researching their family tree can find headstones very useful.

DID YOU KNOW?

- The famous French actress, Sarah Bernhardt, believed in being prepared for death. Years before she died, she bought a coffin which was just the right size for her, and would lie in it for hours pretending to be dead. (Some people claim she even slept in it.) When she wasn't using the coffin herself, Sarah often used it as a drinks table for visitors.

Many old grave inscriptions include little poems or perhaps a Bible verse or saying such as 'not dead, but gone before'. Depending on what the gravestone is made of, and how badly it has weathered, some inscriptions can be difficult to read. A popular stonemason's trick is to insert lead, a soft dark-colored metal, into the carving. This makes the writing easier to read, and less likely to disappear with the years.

Mausoleums are tombs built like little houses, often with a door in the front so that visitors can go inside. (Don't worry, the coffins are safely underground!) As they are large and expensive to build, mausoleums contain several bodies, usually members of the same family.

Many modern Italian families like to build mausoleums, which can include photographs of the people who are buried there. A good example of a cemetery filled with mausoleums can be found on the outskirts of Ingham in North Queensland, where there is a large Italian community.

Star motifs on a grave usually mean that the person buried there was Jewish. A six-pointed star is the symbol of the Jewish religion and people.

Urns, which look like big vases with handles, are a very old symbol of death. They date

> **DID YOU KNOW?**
> • Traditionally, dead people are wrapped up in a long piece of cloth called a shroud or winding sheet. In mediaeval times, the English government passed a law requiring that all people be buried in a shroud made of wool — in order to help the local wool industry!

Stalactites and stalagmites, Royal Cave, Buchan, Victoria, Australia

A smallish example of a Gippsland giant earthworm

One of the largest covered reservoirs in the world (empty in this picture) lies beneath Centennial Park, Sydney, Australia

A stream of molten lava from a volcano

Interior of house in Coober Pedy, Australia
Catacombs: the burial place of the Capuchin monks underneath Rome

Village in Cappadocia, Turkey – half in-ground, half out

Londoners spend the night of 8 October 1940 in the safety of Aldwych Tube station during the German bombing of London, World War II

back to ancient times when the ashes of a dead person were stored in an urn in the family home. Urns in cemeteries do not usually contain the ashes or bones of dead people. They are just there for decoration.

Veils which look like pieces of draped cloth carved in stone can sometimes be seen on tombstones, or draping urns or broken columns. They mean that death 'casts a veil' over the person — in other words, we can no longer see them.

3 People
Underground

Underground homes

Why live underground? Most of us love fresh air and sunlight, the feeling of the wind on our faces, an uninterrupted view of the street or the mountains or the sea. Yet some people deliberately choose to live in homes like caves. There are about 6000 underground homes in North America alone, and many more in other parts of the world like China, where this is a traditional way of building. Funny as it may seem, living underground has many advantages.

The modern fashion for underground homes and buildings started in the early 1970s, when the price of oil suddenly started to rise. In cold climates where indoor heating is necessary, this meant a huge jump in the cost of running a home. A few clever people realized that this problem could be solved by going underground. Underground homes are much easier to heat than normal ones (as long as there is proper insulation) and in hot climates, are extremely cool. They require fewer resources such as timber for building. They are a good choice for scenic areas where the natural beauty would be spoiled by an ordinary house intruding into the landscape. As for lighting, underground homes are not dark and dingy, as you might expect. Most of them have their windows in the ceiling!

In prehistoric times, people took shelter in caves, worshipped their gods there, and sometimes buried their dead in them. Later on, underground villages and cities were built in places like Turkey, Sicily, northern America, and Africa. Living in isolated caves also became popular for holy men and women of different religions in many countries. In the early centuries of Christianity 'hermits' or 'anchorites' as they were called, would often retreat to caves to concentrate on prayer and meditation. The most famous of these hermits was Saint Anthony, who lived to the remarkable age of 105. Unfortunately, his fame spread so quickly that the Egyptian desert surrounding his cave was soon crowded with people wanting to copy him.

> 'hermits' or 'anchorites' ...would often retreat to caves to concentrate on prayer and meditation

Today, the world's most famous underground town is at Coober Pedy in South Australia. (The name Coober Pedy means 'white man's burrows' in the local Aboriginal language.) Coober Pedy is an opal mining town with a particularly harsh climate. It is hot and dry, with summer temperatures often reaching a scorching 122°F. It has no natural water of its own, and no trees suitable for building houses with. The men who went to work there in the early years of this century quickly discovered that it was much cooler in their mines than on the surface. After this discovery, they naturally began building houses underground for coolness and comfort.

House in the rock, Massafra, Italy

Today, with air-conditioners readily and cheaply available, it is not so important for the people of Coober Pedy to live underground. New buildings are often built on the surface — but it is still the underground buildings which the tourists come to see. As well as homes, Coober Pedy has underground shops, motels, and even an underground church!

Underground buildings do not just provide homes for humans. They are also useful for storage, particularly of items which need to be kept cool, at a constant temperature, or safe from attack. Defence organizations keep their weapons in secret underground stores where the enemy will not find them, and where they will be difficult to bomb out or destroy. Fine wines and cheeses are traditionally stored and aged in cellars where the temperature is constant, and film company MGM keeps all its movies in an old salt mine in Kansas for the same reason. In Oxford, the massive Bodleian Library stores miles of books right under the grassy quadrangles of the colleges. And near Salt Lake City, another type of library is located in six enormous underground storage rooms, 820 feet below the surface. Here, the Mormon Church keeps its genealogical records, over 70 million of them. The aim (for religious purposes) is to record as many names as possible, and the huge database is consulted by people all over the world.

> film company MGM keeps all its movies in an old salt mine in Kansas

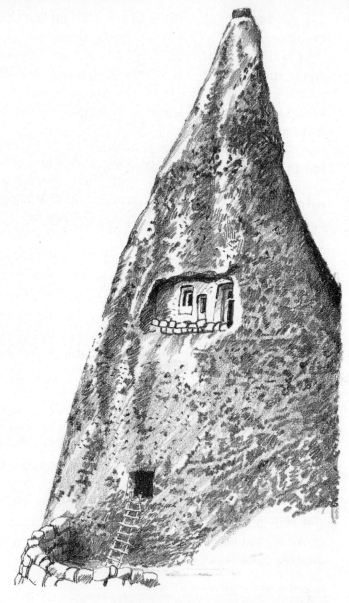

House built into rock, Cappadocia, Turkey

Underground miners

Mining is one of the world's most dangerous and important jobs. Without miners willing to work in the depths of the earth we would have to do without coal for fires and electricity generation, iron for steel-making, gold and silver for jewelry and ornaments and many other things we take for granted.

Mining is the process of digging minerals out of the ground. Minerals are usually found by a geologist, who knows which sort of rocks to look in, and confirms their presence by scientific methods such as core sampling (in which a drill rig bores out narrow 'core' of rock from deep in the earth), and even remote sensing by satellites orbiting the Earth. When the extent of the mineral-bearing rocks is known, engineers work out the best way of mining them. Sometimes the minerals are relatively close to the surface, and an open-cut mine is the best way of digging them up. In open-cut mines, high explosives are used together with huge **draglines** and other earthmoving equipment to lift away the overlying earth, and expose the mineral-bearing rocks underneath. When the minerals are deeply buried, the usual procedure is to dig a deep mine shaft and slowly excavate the rock using cutting machines and explosives.

Working underground is hard, dirty and

> **DID YOU KNOW?**
> • The world's deepest underground mine, listed by *The Guinness Book of Records,* is a gold mine in South Africa, over 2 miles under the earth.

uncomfortable — and it is always dangerous, despite the best efforts of mining companies and engineers. At least most miners today are compensated for their dangerous jobs by good wages and living conditions in the isolated settlements where they often have to work. In earlier centuries, many mine owners did not care whether their workers lived or died. Miners worked long hours in appalling conditions, often

> **Miners worked long hours in appalling conditions, often never seeing the sun**

never seeing the sun. They were paid badly, or in food not money, and often had to take their small children of eight or nine underground to work with them so they could earn enough for the family. Often these children died in explosions or drowned when underground water suddenly filled a shaft. Those who survived to grow up were stunted by the cramped conditions and suffered lung diseases caused by inhaling mine dust. But gradually, responsible mine owners, governments and miners' unions managed to improve conditions. They banned children working underground, improved safety procedures and increased pay to fair and sensible levels.

Mine disasters still occur every year. Mines can flood, ventilation can fail, and mine elevators can collapse. In May 1995, 105 South African gold miners were killed when an elevator plunged 1279 feet to the bottom of a shaft. One particularly deadly combination, common in coal mines, is an explosion (caused by a build-up of coal dust or gases) followed by a cave-in. A serious mine disaster of this type occurred at the Moura coal mine in Australia in August 1994. Despite the best efforts of rescuers the trapped miners could not be freed, and after a second explosion the mine was closed, leaving the men imprisoned forever in their underground tomb.

Underground outlaws

Caves have often provided ready-made shelters for people on the run from the authorities. One outlaw who made the most of a cave hideout was the famous English highwayman, Dick Turpin.

Modern stories about Dick Turpin often make him out to be a very romantic figure, but in real life he was a cruel and vicious man, who once roasted an old lady over her own fire to make her give up her gold wedding ring. With his friend and fellow highwayman, Robert King, Dick Turpin set up a hideout in a cave in Epping Forest, in the English county of Essex. The cave was big enough to hide the highwaymen, their horses (whose tracks they covered by nailing their shoes on backwards) and all their plunder. It was comfortable, and so well hidden by undergrowth that search parties looking for the highwaymen went right past without seeing it on several occasions. In fact, its

> **he was a cruel and vicious man, who once roasted an old lady over her own fire**

Cave hideout used by Pigeon, an Aboriginal outlaw in the Kimberleys

location was not discovered until after Robert King had died, and Dick Turpin had moved to Yorkshire. He was caught and hanged in York in 1739, and the cave became a local tourist attraction.

Other 'outlaws' who hid in caves were not really criminals, but people who were unlucky enough to have displeased the government or important people of the day. When the Roman general Julius Caesar invaded what is now France, many local people hid from his advancing army in caves. This turned out to be a fatal mistake: Caesar ordered his men to block the entrances, and so the people were all buried alive. A similar thing happened at the Cave of Yeermalik in Central Asia during the thirteenth century. When the local people took refuge in the cave, the Mongol leader Genghis Khan tried to smoke them out. When this didn't work, he walled up the entrances and left them to die. In 1840, two English explorers broke into the cave and found hundreds of skeletons lying in the darkness.

Another reason people sometimes hid in caves was to escape religious persecution. The prophet Mohammed, founder of the Islamic religion, hid from his enemies in the Cave of Adullam. In the thirteenth century, a strange sect called the Cathars made a desperate last stand at Montségur Castle in southern France. Shortly before their defeat, the last few Cathars smuggled a mysterious treasure out of the castle into another of their strongholds: a nearby cave. Later the cave was discovered, but it contained only the skeletons of Cathars who had hidden there. The treasure, whatever it was, had vanished.

But perhaps the most notorious outlaws to live in a cave were a Scottish family, the Beans. With his wife and children, Sawney Bean lived undetected in a cave on the coast of Galloway in the seventeenth century for over 20 years. The cave had a narrow, hidden entrance, and turned and twisted into the earth for about one mile. When the tide was high, it filled the mouth so that nobody could enter. For the villainous Beans, it was a perfect lair.

For years, the inhabitants of Galloway were mystified by the way travelers in the area were disappearing. Clearly, some cunning gang of bandits was operating close by, but their victims never escaped to give clues about what was happening. Even stranger, few bodies were ever found. Then, one evening, an hysterical man was brought to the office of the Chief Magistrate in Glasgow, and told a blood-chilling story. He and his wife had been riding home from a local fair when they were attacked, and dragged off their horse by a gang of robbers. As the man watched in horror, his wife was murdered and her body hacked open before his eyes. He was saved from the same brutal treatment by a large party of 20 or 30 riders that scared the attackers off.

For the first time, the Chief Magistrate had a clue to the way the Bean family operated. After seeing the mutilated body of the poor dead woman, he determined to bring her murderers to justice. He wrote a letter to the Scottish King, James VI, telling him the whole story. A few days later, accompanied by the King and 400 armed men, he set off for the forest where the murder had taken place.

The men searched high and low, and at last the bloodhounds they had brought led them to the narrow entrance of a cave. Carrying torches and lanterns, they explored every cranny and side tunnel until at last they came upon the Bean family's hideout. It was a sickening sight. All around were bits of human bodies, dangling from the cave roof, smoking over fires and pickling in barrels. The Bean family had not only murdered the people they robbed: they had been eating them.

Sawney and his wife, their eight sons, six daughters, eighteen grandsons and fourteen granddaughters were all arrested. The 48 murdering Beans were executed in Edinburgh for their crimes — and have passed into Scottish legend.

Fireworks in the cellar

Everybody loves a bonfire and fireworks, and many countries around the world have special days on which firework displays are held. One of the strangest bonfire festivals of all originates in England. Every year, on 5 November English people around the world celebrate Guy Fawkes Night — the anniversary of an underground plot to murder the entire British government.

> **Guy Fawkes Night — the anniversary of an underground plot to murder the government**

Guy Fawkes was born in 1570 in northern England. He was a Roman Catholic who was unhappy with the way Catholics in England were being treated. Guy Fawkes hated the Protestant government which had made Catholic religious services illegal, and longed for the right to practice his own religion. He particularly hated the King, James I, and with a band of fellow conspirators, decided to assassinate him. By blowing up the Houses of Parliament on the day of its

---

UNDERGROUND RECORDS

- Human beings are not designed to live beneath the earth. Shut away from light and air we become ill and mentally disoriented. Experienced cavers recommend that for safety's sake no more than 20 hours at a time should be spent underground.
Needless to say, some people will always want to set records. In 1989, Stefania Follini spent 131 days alone underground in a cave in New Mexico. She broke a record set by France's Véronique le Guen. Véronique spent 111 days alone in a French cave, 262 feet below the ground. She later committed suicide.

opening, the plotters decided, they would not only get rid of the King but the Prince of Wales and 500 Members of Parliament as well.

Although Guy Fawkes is the person who is chiefly remembered today, he was not really a very important member of what is now called the Gunpowder Plot. The chief plotter was a man called Robert Catesby, who was assisted by a number of other Catholics in London and the English Midlands. The plotters' first plan was to dig a tunnel under the Houses of Parliament, but after discovering that the walls there were almost 10 feet thick, they gave this up as hopeless. Instead, they were lucky enough to discover a coal cellar for rent, which was actually underneath the building. Guy Fawkes was put in charge of the cellar. He filled it with 36 deadly barrels of gunpowder, hidden by piles of firewood.

Unfortunately for Guy Fawkes and the other underground plotters, the government was already aware of their plans. Sir Robert Cecil, the Secretary of State, had been informed by his network of spies that something was afoot, and was patiently waiting for the right moment to move in. Late in October 1605, his opportunity arrived. One of the conspirators was becoming anxious about his brother-in-law, Lord Monteagle, who was among the MPs who were about to be blown sky-high. He decided to send him a warning letter, telling him to stay away from Parliament if he valued his life. Lord Monteagle handed the letter straight over to Sir Robert Cecil, and the Gunpowder Plot was exposed.

On the night of 4–5 November 1605, a group of

armed men marched to the Houses of Parliament and broke into the coal cellar. Here they found the 36 barrels of gunpowder and the red-headed, bearded Guy Fawkes, waiting to set off the explosion. Guy Fawkes was arrested and taken off to prison, where on King James' instructions he was tortured to make him reveal the details of the plot. Every day, the torture grew worse, and after four unbearable days, he finally gave away everything he knew. His fellow conspirators were tracked down in the country and arrested after a fierce fight. Those who survived, like Guy Fawkes himself, were eventually tried and executed.

> **Guy Fawkes ... was quickly turned into a sort of bogey-man**

Although the Gunpowder Plotters probably never came close to really blowing up the Houses of Parliament, the people of England were outraged by what had happened. In fact, the plot made conditions for English Catholics worse, not better, for several centuries to come. As for Guy Fawkes, he was quickly turned into a sort of bogey-man. For hundreds of years, on the anniversary of the plot, dummies or 'guys' have been burned on bonfires across the world, while fireworks are set off to celebrate his capture.

Underground warfare

To modern tourists, mediaeval castles look romantic with their towers and moats; but this was not the reason they were built. A castle with its massive stone walls was a lord's stronghold, a place of refuge in times of war and other trouble. Because of this, it was not designed to be beautiful, but incredibly strong.

Mediaeval armies used a number of methods when trying to capture a castle. If an attacking force had enough time, it could cut off the castle's supplies, and starve the people inside into surrendering. It could try and storm the castle with battering rams and siege engines. Or it could resort to a highly specialized underground warfare called mining. While the rest of the army did its best to distract the defenders inside the castle, special troops would start digging mines or tunnels under the massive walls of the castle. Sometimes this was simply to provide a way in for the invaders. In other instances, digging out the foundations was meant to make a section of the castle wall collapse. The miners propped the wall up with wooden posts while they were working to stop it falling in and crushing them. When they were ready to leave, they set fire to the posts. By the time the wood burned through and the wall collapsed, the miners should have had enough time to escape.

special troops would start digging mines or tunnels under the massive walls

Of course, it didn't always work out that way. The miners' tunnel might collapse, or the men might suffocate in the airless passageways before anyone above noticed. The miners also had to work as silently as possible, in case the people inside the castle realized what they were doing. If they did, they would often start digging a countermine or tunnel of their own, hoping to intercept the invaders and kill them. Working in the mines was one of the most dangerous jobs in the army.

Life in the trenches

Another, far deadlier type of underground warfare was carried out in the trenches of World War I. From 1914 to 1918, dug-out networks of tunnels reinforced with sandbags criss-crossed the fields of northern France and Belgium. These tunnels, or trenches formed the line of defence (known as the Western Front) against the invading Germans. Millions of soldiers, including many Australians who were fighting on the Allied (anti-German) side, lived with the constant whine and thud of shells exploding above their heads, never knowing when one would hit and blow everybody to tiny pieces.

> **The only way of seeing out was with a periscope**

Trenches were cold, damp (or wet), and muddy. The only way of seeing out was with a periscope, similar to the ones used on submarines, and even then there was nothing much to look at: only barbed wire, mud and dead bodies. Poison gas attacks by the Germans were a constant danger: a canister of mustard gas thrown into a trench would blind or kill soldiers unlucky enough to be caught without gas masks. From time to time, the men would be ordered to go 'over the top'. Clutching their rifles, they would pour out of the trenches and try to capture nearby German positions — only to be shot down in their thousands by enemy bullets. Over the course of the war, millions of soldiers died on both sides, and many survivors never completely recovered. Years in the trenches, waiting in terror for bombs to fall, gave many soldiers a condition called 'shell shock', which turned them into nervous wrecks for the rest of their lives.

Schoolchildren shelter from falling bombs in a trench during World War II

During World War II (1939-45), underground hiding places were also used as protection against falling bombs: this time by ordinary men, women and children.

In Australia, the only city to be badly bombed (by the Japanese) was Darwin. But in Great Britain, particularly in big cities like London, Birmingham and Coventry, attacks by German bombers happened almost every night. Throughout the famous 'Blitz' of 1940-41, sirens would scream the danger as soon as the first German planes were sighted. Everyone would scramble out of their beds and run outside to hide in special air-raid shelters in their gardens. These underground 'Anderson' shelters were chilly, cramped and often streaming with water. While the bombs rained all around, whole families would huddle together in a covered trench barely 8 feet long, sipping tea, and trying to sleep in uncomfortable triple bunks. (One woman later remembered her family's shelter as being like being buried alive in a 'three-tier coffin'.)

underground hiding places were also used as protection against falling bombs

Of course, rich people could afford bigger and more comfortable shelters. Winston Churchill (the British Prime Minister) and his Cabinet had special underground headquarters near Parliament House. Churchill made many famous radio broadcasts from these 'Cabinet War Rooms', which are now preserved as a museum. (The German leader, Adolf Hitler, shot himself in a similar underground complex in Berlin at the end of the war.) Rich socialites hid in the underground sauna at the posh Dorchester Hotel, while King George VI and his family had a shelter at Buckingham Palace, which was hit several times by German bombs. Mrs. Ella Rowcroft, an eccentric millionaire aged 81, even built herself an underground house, 30 feet below the ground! She installed an elevator to take her down into her shelter, but died of old age before she had a chance to use it.

Poor people, particularly those in heavily bombed areas like London's East End, were not so lucky. Since their tiny terrace houses had no gardens in which to build outdoor shelters, they had to make do with indoor 'Morrisons' which looked like reinforced tables, or rush down the street to the nearest public shelter or underground railway station. Some of the underground public shelters held as many as 15,000 or 20,000 frightened people. (After the war, one of these shelters was used as a TV set for 'Doctor Who', while another, in the London suburb of Finsbury, was turned into an underground parking lot.) Every night the platforms of the railway stations were crammed with people wrapped in blankets and clutching gasmasks — on a single night in September 1940, it was estimated that 117,000 Londoners took refuge in the Tube from German bombs. In disused stations, people even slept on the train tracks!

people even slept on the train tracks!

Hiding out in the Tube was uncomfortable, boring, and sometimes frightening when bombs exploded close by. There were no toilets, only buckets which rapidly became full and smelled so awful that many people preferred to face the danger outside. And while the underground railway stations wcre far deeper than any home shelter, even they were not completely safe. On 15 October 1940, Balham station in London took a direct hit from a German bomb. The ground started collapsing in on the terrified people inside, and water from burst pipes rapidly flooded the tunnels. Sixty-four people were trapped underground and drowned.

Forgotten under the ground

Although the beautiful old castles of Europe look very romantic on postcards, their dungeons were horrible places that make modern prisons look like palaces. They were dank, dark and freezing cold in winter and summer; water often seeped in through the walls from a moat filled with sewage, and there were of course no windows. Small wonder that many prisoners died immediately.

Disgusting as the dungeons were, there was still one sort of underground prison that was worse. One of the most dreaded punishments of all was to be put in a deep, covered pit called an *oubliette*. The name comes from the French word *oublier*, to forget, and once somebody was dropped inside one, that was exactly what happened to them. They were left there on their own in the utter darkness, screaming for help and slowly going mad until they died...

What happens in an underground nuclear test

Everybody has read newspaper reports and seen television bulletins about underground nuclear tests in places like China and Mururoa Atoll in the South Pacific. Many people in countries around the world have been angered by them. But what actually happens in an underground nuclear test? And why are nuclear bombs exploded underground at all?

Nuclear weapons are among the most dangerous ever created by human beings. Depending on how close a person is to a nuclear explosion, he or she can simply vaporize (vanish like a puff of smoke), be fried to a crisp, or die horribly from radiation. Exposure to radiation also causes diseases like cancer which can affect a survivor years after the explosion happened. In Japan, people who survived the American nuclear bomb attacks on Nagasaki and Hiroshima are still dying as a result of explosions which happened in 1945.

> **people...are still dying as a result of explosions which happened in 1945**

From time to time, governments which possess nuclear bombs decide they want to test them. In the early days of nuclear weapons, these tests were usually done in the open air. The American government practiced letting off bombs in the Nevada desert, and even encouraged people to come and watch from ridges at a 'safe' distance of about 6 miles away. Of course, there was nothing safe about these tests at all. Radioactive material was carried by the wind in every direction, and gradually, the scientists in charge of these projects realized that their tests were endangering people and wildlife. They decided to find an alternative, safer way of testing the bombs, and put them underground.

The fact is that nuclear weapons are never really safe. However, an underground nuclear test is certainly not as dangerous as one held in the open air. The immediate **fallout** is many times less, and the explosion is more contained. The nuclear device is always buried very deeply — perhaps 3281 feet or more below the surface — and after the explosion the radiation is trapped beneath the earth. Governments with bombs often use these facts as excuses to let them off.

When the decision has been taken to test a nuclear bomb underground, and the supervising scientists have made their own preparations, a drill rig similar to the ones used by mining companies digs a bore hole at the test site. (These are usually in isolated places like deserts, or in the case of Mururoa Atoll, an uninhabited island in the Pacific Ocean.) The bomb and monitoring instruments are lowered into the hole and more monitoring instruments are set up for miles all around. The area is evacuated and the nuclear device is detonated.

On the surface, the ground rises and collapses back very quickly, leaving a depression. A huge pressure wave spreads out

A huge pressure wave spreads out underground

underground from the explosion, and the intense heat which is generated vaporizes a hole deep in the ground. The size of the pressure wave and the hole depends on how big the bomb was. Nuclear bombs are measured according to their equivalent in dynamite, so a 100,000 ton bomb has the same effect as 100,000 tons of dynamite being exploded all at once. In earthquake terms, that's like a quake measuring 6 on the Richter Scale. An explosion like this can be felt 62 miles away, and can be measured on **seismometers** all around the world.

The heat from a nuclear explosion doesn't just vaporize the rock under the ground. It also melts a layer of rock around the hole, which turns into a sort of glassy super-rock. Beyond the layer of glassy rock there is a zone of intense cracking, which gradually disappears further away from the source of the explosion.

Scientists who perform nuclear tests claim that the layer of glassy rock which surrounds the hole acts as a seal, and shuts all the radiation safely away underground. However, other people are not so sure. They are not convinced that the glassy rock will hold in the radiation, and are afraid that in the long term water might penetrate through the cracks and become contaminated. If this contaminated water seeps into ground water, it may become a real risk to people in the future. At Mururoa Atoll, the French government has let off so many underground bombs that the structure of the underlying rocks is probably badly damaged. Many environmentalists are worried that radiation might some day leak out into the sea.

4 Underground Buildings and Tunnels

Trains beneath the Earth

In the early days of the railways, traveling by train was often dangerous. Terrible accidents would happen, often because the new railway technology was too primitive, or not properly understood. One of the most nerve-wracking moments in any railway journey always came when a train approached a tunnel.

Today, people think nothing of going through a tunnel. Most of us even think it's rather fun, especially when the tunnel is a long one which passes through a mountain. But 150 years ago when steam trains were new and terrifying, railway tunnels were an altogether different matter. As the train disappeared into the darkness, the noise of its engines became hideously loud. Choking clouds of steam and smoke filled the air, and all the passengers would tense up, waiting anxiously for the first sign of daylight. Anything could happen in the darkness. The train could break down, and nobody would know, or perhaps it would run into a rockfall. Worst of all, it might meet another train coming in the opposite direction, and there would be an appalling accident underneath the earth.

Early train drivers had no radios, or any other way

**Anything could happen
in the darkness**

of making contact with the
nearest station or signal box. Once they entered a tunnel,
they could see nothing ahead of them, and there was no
way for the outside world to warn them of any danger. In
order to minimize the chance of one train running into
another in the darkness, many tunnels had manned
signal boxes, one at each end. A stop signal flipped up
automatically when a train entered the tunnel, and the
signal operators would send telegraph messages
between the boxes, letting each other know when trains
entered and left. The rule they followed was as simple as
it was important. Only one train was supposed to be in
the tunnel at any time.

In August 1861, a signaling set-up like this existed
at the Clayton Tunnel, on England's busy London to
Brighton line. One Sunday morning, three steam trains
were scheduled to pass in quick succession. The first
train, which had left Brighton at 8.28 A.M., went safely
through the tunnel, but for some reason, the stop signal
failed to pop up when it entered at the southern end. A
bell rang in the signalman's office, but he was tired and
overworked after 24 hours on the job and didn't notice.
By the time the next train came through less than two
minutes later, he barely had time to wave his emergency
red flag at its driver.

The red flag meant that the driver of the second

train was supposed to stop, so this is what he did —
inside the tunnel. Meanwhile, a message had been
telegraphed back from the signal box at the other end,
the northern end, saying that the tunnel was clear. This
message actually meant that the *first* train had steamed
out into the daylight, but the poor tired southern
signalman assumed it referred to both the first and the
second. By this time, a third train had arrived, so he
waved it on into the tunnel. This last train was an
express, and traveling very fast; its driver had no idea
that another train was already waiting in the darkness.
Even worse, the other train was now going... backwards!

The driver of the second train had just glimpsed
the emergency red flag as he drove into the tunnel. He
knew it probably meant that a train or other obstacle
was ahead, so he decided to go back and ask the

signalman what was wrong.

> **Deep inside the earth, the two trains collided**

Unfortunately, he never got the
chance. Deep inside the earth,
the two trains collided. Twenty-
one people were killed and 176 were injured in one of
nineteenth-century England's most horrifying railway
accidents.

Despite the Clayton Tunnel accident, English
people lost none of their enthusiasm for traveling by
train. In fact, it was about the same time that they started
developing the very first complete underground rail
system: the London Underground, or Tube. In big cities
with congested streets and lots of traffic, underground
trains make a lot of sense. Underground trains take up
little valuable space, are not noisy, and create few traffic

hazards. Since the London Tube was opened in 1863, countless cities across the world have followed suit.

The London Underground was the brainchild of a far-sighted man called Charles Pearson. For almost 20 years, he campaigned to have the railways taken underground, and although there were many problems with his idea (including the question of what to do with the steam train's smoke) he eventually found enough people willing to invest the money that was needed.

The first underground train link in London (now known as the Metropolitan line) took three years to build. A special steam engine with a smoke tank was designed for underground use (the smoke was later released into the open through two special chimneys disguised as houses), and the new venture was launched with free trips, and a grand party. Sadly, Charles Pearson had not lived to see his Underground become a reality, but the idea caught on, and over the following decades, more and more tunnels were built. Clean electric trains that didn't make lots of smoke were introduced in 1890. Today, the London Underground is the largest and most famous underground rail system in the world, carrying 735 million passengers a year.

Sensational sewers

Think about going to the toilet. Every time we pull the chain or push the flush button, the toilet has to empty somewhere. Most people know that 'black water' (as the bowl contents are called) goes into the sewer, a huge drainpipe which runs under the street and takes it away for treatment. Today we take toilets and sewers for granted. But in earlier times people went to the toilet wherever they happened to be at the time: a habit which was smelly and also unhealthy.

The idea of sending toilet waste underground was probably an Indian one. Nearly 5000 years ago, the people of Mohenjo Daro in northern India came up with a brilliant idea: U-shaped brick sewers under most of their streets, which flowed away into special holding pits called **cesspools.** From time to time, when they filled up and the smell got too bad, the cesspools would be cleaned out, then people could start filling them up all over again. Archaeologists have also found what might be a sewer system at the village of Skara Brae, on a remote island off the coast of Scotland. The villagers of Skara Brae built toilets which emptied into underground sewers and eventually flowed over a cliff into the North Sea.

The best sewer-builders of ancient times were the Romans. The Romans were very fussy about cleanliness, and wherever they established towns they built public toilets with complicated drainage systems to take away the waste. Some of these Roman sewers were so well built that they are still in use today. One of these, the main sewer in the city of Rome, was built around 2,600 years ago and called the *cloaca maxima* or 'big drain'. The walls were made of three layers of wedge-shaped stones. It was 12 feet deep, and just over 20 feet across (about as wide as many suburban streets). But as with all sewage systems, the biggest problem was where the sewage should be disposed of. The Romans solved the problem by emptying the *cloaca maxima* straight into the River Tiber. Since plenty of clean fresh water was piped in daily from the hills surrounding the city, this was not such a health risk as it would have been if people were using the river water to drink and wash in. All the same, in hot summer weather the Tiber was infamous as one of the smelliest rivers in the world.

By the Middle Ages the idea of having **breeding grounds for all sorts of deadly diseases** underground sewage systems had disappeared again, except in a few monasteries (monks and nuns tended to be cleaner than the rest of the population). Most people were happy to use chamberpots, which were emptied out of the window with a warning shout to give passers-by enough time to duck out of the way. Instead of sewers, mediaeval towns had open drains called kennels which ran down the middle of their streets into cesspools. These cesspools were breeding grounds for all sorts of deadly diseases. People occasionally fell into them, too. In 1326 a cesspool cleaner called Richard the Raker slipped through the planks while cleaning out a public toilet, and drowned in the sewage before anyone could fish him out.

To modern people, used to clean toilets and underground drainage, living like this seems unbelievably disgusting. Yet as recently as 150 years ago, a city as big as London was not completely sewered. There were no public toilets and people who needed one simply went into the nearest alleyway and squatted on the ground. Not surprisingly, in the late 1850s London suffered from a curious problem called the 'Great Stink'. The Great Stink was caused by untreated sewage flowing through the city's sewers into the River Thames. One sewer in Westminster, near the Houses of Parliament, was particularly disgusting. (In fact, the Great Stink was so awful all the M.P.s had to be evacuated.) Workers who went underground to investigate the problem found a slowly moving tide of sewage which included blood and animal insides from local slaughterhouses, dead dogs, cats, and rats. Worst of all were the 3 feet-long stalactites of black, scummy sludge which hung from the sewer roof and brushed against the faces and bodies of unwary workers.

Today London, like most other modern cities around the world, has a sanitary sewage treatment system. Networks of pipes take sewage away to treatment plants where it is purified so that it can be released safely into the environment. But from time to time, it is still necessary to send workers down into sewers and stormwater drains to inspect them and carry out routine maintenance. Modern councils and water authorities are very aware that sewers (especially old ones) are dangerous places, and that serious and even fatal accidents can occur in them. Workers can easily slip, or be overcome by poisonous sewer gas, which forms when organic matter in the sewer decays. And unless they are vaccinated by doctors, they can catch life-threatening diseases like tetanus or hepatitis from the sewer's contents.

Modern sewer workers are trained to cope with all sorts of emergencies underground. They are supplied with sophisticated safety equipment such as closed-circuit televisions (to inspect sewers which are too narrow to crawl into) and gas detectors to check for poisonous or flammable gases. Gas detectors can be lowered into the sewer through a manhole, or strapped to the worker's chest. If the atmosphere becomes dangerous, an alarm goes off, and everyone in the sewer beats a hasty retreat. And if there is an emergency — for example if somebody is overcome by gas — rescuers equipped with breathing apparatus can find them, and winch them to the surface using a lifeline and an electric windlass.

It is hard to imagine that many people would line up for a job working in a

clubs of 'drain explorers'

sewer. Strange as it may seem though, there are some people who actually enjoy going down into sewers — and do it on weekends as a hobby! In some cities, clubs of 'drain explorers' (many of whom are also keen cavers) explore train tunnels, storm-water drains and other underground hiding places found beneath the streets in modern cities. It is a dangerous hobby, and probably often a smelly one. But for the people who do it, even the dankest, darkest drainpipe can be an underground adventure.

Treasures in the trash

Archaeologists often seem to have a very glamorous life. They travel to far-off exciting places like Egypt and Greece and spend their lives looking for buried treasure. Ancient buildings, long-forgotten tombs, even whole cities sleep beneath the earth, waiting for someone to come and find them. And hidden in the dust, with the pots and bones and houses of people who lived before us, an enticing gleam of gold beckons the sharp-eyed treasure-hunter onwards.

Early archaeologists really were little better than treasure-seekers, out to find as much ancient gold as they could. It took many years for people to realize that the most valuable treasure was often the stuff which looked like junk — everyday items which ancient people had worn out and thrown away. Today, the most important part of any archaeological dig is often the garbage dump. Garbage from ancient houses can tell us what people ate and how they cooked it, what they wore, and how they went about their everyday lives. And since one of the main ways of getting rid of garbage is to bury it, there are always plenty of long-forgotten junk heaps for archaeologists to look at.

Like ancient people, modern societies also bury their garbage to get it out of the way — an enormous amount of it every year. This underground waste is known as landfill. Finding safe, cheap, convenient places to bury it is a huge headache for governments all over the Western world.

Archaeologists of the future will probably thank twentieth-century people for leaving so much wonderful garbage for them to dig through. And in fact, the digging has already started. 'Urban archaeologists' who specialize in the study of

> sludgy remains of TV dinners

modern societies instead of ancient ones have begun to turn to the thousands of landfill sites which dot the planet. Gleefully, they ferret through old papers, food packages and electrical goods, and sift through the

83

sludgy remains of TV dinners, take-out hamburgers and used disposable diapers. By studying the remains of the average family's trash, the garbage archaeologists can learn more about the way modern society works — what we eat, what we buy and how we spend our leisure time. They also hope to be able to advise governments and local councils on the best way of dealing with our horrendous waste problem.

The Garbage Project from the University of Arizona has been operating for over 20 years, and has made some intriguing discoveries about the sort of things modern people throw out. For example, there is more paper, especially newspaper, in landfill than anything else. Plastic packing squashes down and is not nearly as big a problem as most of us think, nor are disposable diapers (in America, babies poo their way through 1,600 million diapers every year). Garbage Project Director William Rathje is always fascinated by the things he finds in American landfills, but he is also disgusted by the waste of things like paper which could easily be recycled. Strangely enough, edible food always makes up a big percentage of any excavation. Because the rubbish is deeply buried and cut off from the outside air, hardly any of it rots down. Rathje and his team of students have even found 25-year-old hotdogs, perfectly preserved! — as well as 40-year-old phone directories that can still be read. Of course they smell; garbage archaeologists wear masks at work.

One strange thing about landfills is the way tires keep rising to the top, like rice in boiling water. This happens because of the pressure from garbage trucks

25-year-old hotdogs, perfectly preserved!

passing over the surface. One day all the tires are collected; next day more pop up.

Landfills are big business. One of the largest is Fresh Kills Landfill, New York, which is 25 times the size of the Great Pyramid in Egypt. In the United States, huge bucket augurs drill holes in landfill sites to get access to the methane gas which is generated by garbage as it rots. This gas can be sold for use as a fuel. People *can* get money from rubbish; treasure from trash.

5 Legends of Darkness

The monster in the maze

There was once a king of Crete called Minos who had a terrible secret. His wife, the beautiful Pasiphae, had given birth to a monster, a hideous creature that was half man, half bull. The monster was known as the Minotaur, and since it had been sent as a punishment by the gods, Minos knew he could not get rid of it. Instead, he called on the legendary architect, Daedalus, to build him a labyrinth: an immense underground maze, where the Minotaur could be hidden away from sight.

For years, the Minotaur lived in the dark and lonely tunnels under the palace at Knossos, the Cretan capital. From time to time, its anguished bellowing could be heard in the painted corridors of the king's apartments; the earth would rumble, and everyone trembled and dreaded what might happen if it escaped. To keep the monster happy, Minos would occasionally feed it human flesh. Every year fourteen young men and women would arrive in Knossos from the kingdom of Athens. One by one, the terrified victims would be pushed into the labyrinth, to wander about lost in the darkness until the Minotaur found and ate them...

terrified victims would be pushed into the labyrinth

The Athenians hated having to send their sons and daughters away to be eaten, but because the Cretans were more powerful than they were, they had no choice. Eventually, the Athenian king's son Theseus decided it was time to do something. Despite his father's attempts to stop him, Prince Theseus sailed to Knossos with the rest of the victims. Here he was lucky enough to meet King Minos' daughter, Ariadne. She fell in love with him, and promised to help him defeat the monster.

When the time came for Theseus to be fed to the Minotaur, Ariadne left a sword and a ball of wool just inside the entrance to the maze. Theseus tied the wool to a rock at the entrance, and strode boldly off along the passage, unraveling the ball as he went.

The labyrinth was dark and musty. Some of the passages were barely wide enough to turn around in. Everything stank of death and decay, and from time to time, Theseus stumbled over gnawed bones and scraps of clothing, left behind after the Minotaur had devoured his previous victims.

Eventually, after many wrong turnings and long hours in the darkness, Theseus reached the heart of the labyrinth. He found the Minotaur waiting for him, and after a fierce struggle, he killed it. Then, using the trail of wool to guide him, he retraced his steps to the entrance where Ariadne was waiting for him. The power of the underground monster was broken forever.

mazes and underground rooms were very common in ancient religions

The story of Theseus' underground battle is just a legend. However, like many myths, it does have some basis in truth. Although nobody has ever satisfactorily identified the Minotaur's labyrinth, we do know that mazes and underground rooms were very common in ancient religions. The Cretans would have used the labyrinth for processions, and perhaps for sacrifices. We know that their religion often involved bull worship, so this may be where the story of the Minotaur came from.

One particularly unusual ritual which may have taken place at the heart of the labyrinth was 'bull-leaping'. A famous wall painting at Knossos shows young men and women performing gymnastics — on the back of a charging bull! The 'bull-leapers' ran towards the bull, grabbed it by the horns, and somersaulted up onto its back and off again. This would have been incredibly dangerous, but the leapers probably felt the risk to their lives was worth it. Even today, people in southern Europe happily participate in bull-fights and bull-running, knowing they may be gored to death. In fact, Spanish and French bull-fights may even be descended from the ancient Cretan rituals shown on the walls of the Knossos palace.

Round trips to Hades

Another fascinating story about an ancient underground complex comes from ancient Rome. According to the Greeks and Romans, when a person died, his or her spirit went to Hades, the world of the dead or Underworld. The Underworld was literally 'under' the earth, and old legends told how brave people would occasionally venture there on a quest or mission. One famous visitor was the musician Orpheus, who went to rescue the spirit of his dead wife, Eurydice. Another was the mythical Trojan hero Aeneas, whose descendants later founded Rome.

The Romans agreed that the entrance to the Underworld was located on Mount Avernus, a real volcano on Italy's western coast. (It is part of the same volcanic region as Mount Vesuvius, the volcano which destroyed Pompeii.) Mount Avernus was also famous for its Sibyl: an ancient, weird old woman who lived in a cave and would foretell the future to people who were brave enough to visit her. Aeneas was one of them. According to the story, the Sibyl gave him directions on how to reach the Underworld, where he hoped to learn about his future destiny.

In the early 1960s, two former naval officers with an interest in ancient history started wondering whether or not there was something in the story. Together, Robert Paget and Keith Jones started exploring the slopes of the volcano, concentrating their efforts on the many caverns and crannies in the area. Eventually, after two years of searching, they discovered an amazing underground complex of tunnels which nobody had ever guessed existed.

Although, like most volcanic regions, Avernus was riddled with natural tunnels made by lava flows, the passages the two explorers discovered were made by humans. Nobody really knows why. However, they seem to have been used by the priests of a nearby temple for religious purposes, perhaps to consult the dead for oracles. Just like Aeneas, visitors would be escorted down 656 feet of long, dimly lit tunnels, barely wide enough to take a single person, to a secret sanctuary hidden in the depths of the earth. Many people who visited must have hoped to catch sight of long-dead relatives. Others, like Aeneas, may have wanted to learn about the future.

What did the visitors to Hades see when they arrived at the end of the tunnel? First they encountered a boiling hot underground river (fed by volcanic springs, similar to those at Rotarua in New Zealand). This was the 'River Styx', which dead souls had to cross in a ferry boat to reach the Underworld. We don't know what they saw after that. The people who visited the tunnels under Mount Avernus have taken the secret to their graves.

> the 'River Styx', which dead souls had to cross in a ferry boat to reach the Underworld

The magician in the cave

One of the most famous people who lived in a cave — even if scholars still argue about whether he ever existed — is King Arthur's friend and adviser, Merlin the Magician. Legends tell us how Merlin took the baby king away from his parents at Tintagel Castle in Cornwall, England, and brought him up in a cave hidden deep in the woods. This cave was Merlin's home, and the heart of all his magic. Later, when Arthur was king and the magician grew tired of life at the castle of Camelot, he would disappear back to his cave for months, or even years, and neither Arthur nor his Knights of the Round Table could find him.

When Merlin grew old, he fell in love with a beautiful young witch called Nimue. Nimue tricked

she left him sleeping in a magical crystal cave

Merlin into teaching her all his magic. When she knew everything, she imprisoned the magician with his own spells and left him sleeping in a magical crystal cave in the forest of Broceliande. Some stories about King Arthur claim that he too lies sleeping in a magic cave, waiting with his knights to rescue Britain in its darkest hour. And to this day, visitors to Tintagel on the wild, rocky coast of western England are shown a mysterious cave in the rocks at the foot of the cliff — where, legends say, Merlin the magician used to live.

Glossary

bacteria: microscopic organisms or "germs" which feed on living or dead matter and help break it down

cesspool: a deep pit dug to collect and hold raw sewage

coffins and caskets: containers for burying bodies in. A casket is rectangular, a coffin bulges out around the shoulders.

crater: a depression with raised sides at the top of a volcano, sometimes containing a lake

crypt: an underground room for burying bodies in, often found under old churches and cathedrals

dragline: a large piece of earthmoving equipment used in open cut mining. It has a huge scoop which is dragged across the mine floor to collect mineral bearing rocks and earth.

fallout: radioactive dust and material found in the air after a nuclear explosion

seismometer: a device used to measure earthquakes and other tremors in the earth from many miles away

sexton: the person who runs and takes care of a cemetery

shroud: a special cloth used for wrapped dead bodies in (sometimes called a winding sheet)

sonar: a way of measuring distance by bouncing sound waves off solid objects

undertaker: a person who prepares a dead body for burial or cremation, and helps relatives make arrangements for the funeral

Reading List

The following books will help you find out more about caves, graves, catacombs and other underground places.

Mine Work
by Donna Bailey
(Heinemann Educational, Oxford, 1991)

Earthquakes and Volcanoes
by Basil Booth
(Evans, London, 1985)

Cave Life
by Christine Gunzi
(Angus & Robertson, Sydney, 1993)

Cave
by Brian Knapp
(Macmillan, Melbourne, 1992)

Volcanoes: Fire from the Earth
by Maurice Krafft
(Thames & Hudson, London, 1993)

Earthquakes and Volcanoes
by David Lambert
(Wayland, Hove, 1985)

Australian Bats
by Jill Morris
(Greater Glider Publications, Maleny, 1993)

The War Years: The Home Front
by Brian Moses
(Wayland, Hove, 1995)

Bog Bodies
by Natalie Jane Prior
(Allen & Unwin, Sydney, 1993)

Mysterious Ruins, Lost Cities and Buried Treasure
by Natalie Jane Prior
(Allen & Unwin, Sydney, 1994)

Cave
by Donald M. Silver
(Freeman, New York, 1993)

If you have access to the Internet, you might like to visit 'Volcano World', and find out about all the latest volcanic eruptions. Its location is:

http://volcano.und.nodak.edu/learning.html

Index